Kiwi Jam Delights

A Flavorful Journey through Kiwi-Inspired Preserves

KIWI JAM DELIGHTS

First edition. January 28, 2024.

ISBN: 979-8224458585

Written by Jose Maria.

Table of Contents

Jose Maria

❖ Introduction:

Welcome to the World of Kiwi Jams
Brief History of Kiwi Fruit:

Kiwi, originally known as the Chinese gooseberry, has a fascinating history dating back to its origins in China. Introduced to the world in the early 20th century, this small, fuzzy fruit quickly gained popularity for its unique taste and vibrant green color. New Zealand later adopted and cultivated the fruit, renaming it the kiwi after their national bird. Over the years, kiwi has become a global sensation, celebrated for its sweet and tart flavor profile, as well as its numerous health benefits.

Why Kiwi Jam is Special:

Kiwi jam is a delightful and versatile creation that captures the essence of this exotic fruit in a spreadable form. The vibrant green hue and bold flavor of kiwi make it an exciting addition to the world of preserves. What sets kiwi jam apart is its perfect balance of sweetness and tartness, creating a taste experience that is both refreshing and indulgent.

Beyond its delicious taste, kiwi jam offers a variety of culinary possibilities. Whether enjoyed on toast, paired with cheese, or used as a filling for pastries, the versatility of kiwi jam makes it a kitchen essential. Additionally, the nutritional benefits of kiwi, packed with vitamin C, fiber, and antioxidants, make this jam a healthier alternative to many commercially available spreads.

Join us on a Flavorful Journey through Kiwi-Inspired Preserves, as we explore the nuances of creating the perfect kiwi jam, from selecting the finest fruits to crafting innovative variations that will tantalize your taste buds. Let's embark on this delicious adventure together!

Chapter 1: Getting Started with Kiwi Jams

1.1 Choosing the Right Kiwis

Before diving into the world of kiwi jams, mastering the art of selecting the right kiwis is paramount. The key to a successful jam lies in the quality of your ingredients.

Selecting Ripe Kiwi Fruits:

Look for Plumpness: Choose kiwis that feel plump and yield slightly to gentle pressure. This indicates ripeness without being overly soft.

Consistent Color: Opt for fruits with a vibrant green color. Avoid overly ripe kiwis with a yellowish tint or overly firm ones that may need more time to ripen.

Fragrance: A sweet and slightly floral fragrance near the stem end is a sign of a ripe kiwi. Avoid any sour or fermented smells.

Understanding Different Kiwi Varieties:

Green Kiwi (Actinidia deliciosa): The classic choice, known for its emerald-green flesh and a perfect balance of sweetness and tartness.

Gold Kiwi (Actinidia chinensis): Recognized by its golden flesh and a sweeter taste than the green variety. It adds a delightful sweetness to your jam.

Baby Kiwi (Hardy Kiwi): Petite and smooth-skinned, these small kiwis offer a concentrated flavor and are perfect for unique jam combinations.

Red Kiwi (Actinidia melanandra): A rare variety with a vibrant red or purple flesh, lending a visually stunning and distinct flavor to your jams.

Experimenting with a combination of these varieties can elevate your jam to new heights, providing a nuanced and complex flavor profile.

1.2 Essential Equipment and Ingredients

Now that you've selected the perfect kiwis, let's gather the tools and ingredients needed to embark on your kiwi jam-making journey.

Kitchen Tools Needed for Jam-Making:

Large Pot or Jam Pan: For cooking the jam mixture evenly.

Wooden Spoon: Ideal for stirring and preventing the jam from sticking to the pan.

Canning Jars with Lids: To store and preserve your kiwi jam.

Canning Funnel: Facilitates easy and mess-free pouring of jam into jars.

Ladle: For transferring the hot jam into jars.

Jar Lifter: Helps safely place and remove jars from boiling water during the canning process.

Kitchen Thermometer: Ensures accurate temperature control for achieving the desired jam consistency.

Key Ingredients for Kiwi Jams:

Ripe Kiwis: As you've meticulously selected earlier.

Granulated Sugar: A sweetener essential for preserving the jam and enhancing its taste.

Pectin: A natural thickening agent that helps achieve the desired jam consistency.

Lemon Juice: Adds acidity, brightens flavor, and helps with the jam's setting.

Optional Flavor Enhancers: Depending on your recipe, you might include ingredients like lime, berries, jalapeños, or chia seeds for unique twists.

Now that you're well-equipped, let the jam-making adventure begin! In the next sections, we'll explore basic kiwi jam recipes and creative variations to delight your taste buds.

Chapter 2: Basic Kiwi Jam Recipes

2.1 Classic Kiwi Jam
Simple Recipe for Traditional Kiwi Jam
Ingredients:

- 4 cups peeled and diced ripe kiwis
- 3 cups granulated sugar
- 1/4 cup lemon juice
- 1 package (1.75 oz) fruit pectin

Instructions:

1. In a large pot, combine the diced kiwis and lemon juice. Stir in the pectin until well mixed.
2. Place the pot over medium-high heat and bring the kiwi mixture to a full boil, stirring frequently.
3. Once boiling, add the granulated sugar all at once, stirring continuously. Return the mixture to a rapid boil and let it boil for 1-2 minutes until the sugar is fully dissolved.
4. Test the jam's consistency by placing a small amount on a cold plate. If it wrinkles and holds its shape when touched, it's ready.
5. Remove the pot from heat and skim off any foam from the surface.
6. Ladle the hot jam into sterilized jars, leaving about 1/4-inch headspace. Wipe the jar rims, place sterilized lids, and screw on the bands until fingertip-tight.
7. Process the jars in a boiling water bath for 10 minutes to ensure proper sealing.
8. Allow the jars to cool completely before checking the seals. Store in a cool, dark place.

Tips for Perfecting the Set:

- Use ripe but not overly soft kiwis for the best flavor and texture.
- Ensure the sugar is completely dissolved before reaching a rapid boil.
- Regularly stir the mixture to prevent it from sticking to the pot.
- Perform a cold plate test to determine the jam's setting point.

2.2 Kiwi Lime Fusion Jam
Adding a Citrusy Twist to Your Jams
Ingredients:

- 3 cups peeled and diced ripe kiwis
- 1 cup peeled and diced fresh lime segments
- 3 cups granulated sugar
- 1/4 cup lime juice
- 1 package (1.75 oz) fruit pectin

Complementary Flavor Combinations:

- For an extra zing, add a tablespoon of finely grated lime zest during cooking.
- Incorporate a hint of fresh mint or basil for a herbal undertone.
- Consider a small amount of ginger for a subtle warmth.

Instructions:

1. Follow the same steps as the Classic Kiwi Jam recipe, substituting lime segments for a portion of the kiwis and adding lime juice for an extra burst of citrus flavor.
2. Experiment with complementary flavors by adding optional ingredients during the boiling process.
3. Continue with the remaining steps for jar filling and processing.

Tips for Complementary Flavor Combinations:

- Adjust the amount of lime juice according to your taste preferences.
- Taste the jam during cooking and add complementary flavors gradually to achieve the desired balance.
- Let the jam sit for a day before consuming to allow the flavors to meld.

These basic kiwi jam recipes lay the foundation for your flavorful journey. Feel free to explore and modify based on your taste preferences!

Chapter 3: Creative Kiwi Jam Variations

3.1 Spicy Kiwi Jalapeño Jam
A Kick of Heat to Elevate Your Jam Experience
Ingredients:

- 4 cups peeled and diced ripe kiwis
- 1 cup finely chopped fresh jalapeños (seeds removed for milder heat)
- 3 cups granulated sugar
- 1/4 cup lemon juice
- 1 package (1.75 oz) fruit pectin

Instructions:

1. In a large pot, combine the diced kiwis, chopped jalapeños, and lemon juice. Stir in the pectin until well mixed.
2. Place the pot over medium-high heat and bring the kiwi mixture to a full boil, stirring frequently.
3. Once boiling, add the granulated sugar all at once, stirring continuously. Return the mixture to a rapid boil and let it boil for 1-2 minutes until the sugar is fully dissolved.
4. Test the jam's consistency by placing a small amount on a cold plate. If it wrinkles and holds its shape when touched, it's ready.
5. Remove the pot from heat and skim off any foam from the surface.
6. Ladle the hot jam into sterilized jars, leaving about 1/4-inch headspace. Wipe the jar rims, place sterilized lids, and screw on the bands until fingertip-tight.
7. Process the jars in a boiling water bath for 10 minutes to ensure proper sealing.
8. Allow the jars to cool completely before checking the seals.

Store in a cool, dark place.

Serving Suggestions for Spicy Kiwi Jam:

- Spread over cream cheese and serve with crackers for a delicious appetizer.
- Use as a glaze for grilled chicken or pork.
- Add a dollop to your favorite tacos or nachos for a sweet and spicy twist.

3.2 Kiwi Berry Bliss Jam
Incorporating Other Fruits for a Delightful Blend
Ingredients:

- 3 cups peeled and diced ripe kiwis
- 1 cup mixed berries (such as strawberries, blueberries, and raspberries), finely chopped
- 3 cups granulated sugar
- 1/4 cup lemon juice
- 1 package (1.75 oz) fruit pectin

Experimenting with Mixed-Berry Combinations:

- Try equal parts of strawberries, blueberries, and raspberries for a balanced berry flavor.
- Adjust the berry ratio to your liking, experimenting with different combinations.

Instructions:

1. Follow the same steps as the Classic Kiwi Jam recipe, adding the mixed berries along with the kiwis during the cooking process.
2. Ensure the berries are finely chopped to distribute their flavors evenly.

3. Continue with the remaining steps for jar filling and processing.

Tips for Mixed-Berry Combinations:

- Adjust the sugar quantity based on the sweetness of the berries.
- Consider adding a splash of balsamic vinegar for depth and complexity.
- Experiment with different berry combinations to find your perfect blend.

These creative kiwi jam variations offer a spicy and fruity twist to your jam collection. Explore the bold flavors and discover new ways to enjoy these unique creations!

Chapter 4: Special Occasion Kiwi Jam Creations

4.1 Kiwi Champagne Jam
Elevate Your Celebrations with a Touch of Elegance
Ingredients:

- 3 cups peeled and diced ripe kiwis
- 1 1/2 cups champagne or sparkling wine
- 3 cups granulated sugar
- 1/4 cup lemon juice
- 1 package (1.75 oz) fruit pectin

Instructions:

1. In a large pot, combine the diced kiwis, champagne, and lemon juice. Stir in the pectin until well mixed.
2. Place the pot over medium-high heat and bring the kiwi mixture to a full boil, stirring frequently.
3. Once boiling, add the granulated sugar all at once, stirring continuously. Return the mixture to a rapid boil and let it boil for 1-2 minutes until the sugar is fully dissolved.
4. Test the jam's consistency by placing a small amount on a cold plate. If it wrinkles and holds its shape when touched, it's ready.
5. Remove the pot from heat and skim off any foam from the surface.
6. Ladle the hot jam into sterilized jars, leaving about 1/4-inch headspace. Wipe the jar rims, place sterilized lids, and screw on the bands until fingertip-tight.
7. Process the jars in a boiling water bath for 10 minutes to ensure proper sealing.
8. Allow the jars to cool completely before checking the seals.

Store in a cool, dark place.

Pairing Ideas for Kiwi Champagne Jam:

- Spread on freshly baked croissants for a luxurious breakfast or brunch.
- Serve alongside a cheese platter with brie or camembert for an elegant appetizer.
- Use as a filling for macarons or thumbprint cookies for a sophisticated dessert.

4.2 Kiwi Jam-filled Pastries
Using Kiwi Jam as a Delicious Pastry Filling
Ingredients:

- Puff pastry sheets (store-bought or homemade)
- Kiwi jam (from any of the previous recipes)
- Powdered sugar for dusting (optional)

Instructions:

1. Preheat your oven according to the puff pastry package instructions.
2. Roll out the puff pastry sheets on a lightly floured surface.
3. Cut the pastry into squares or rectangles, depending on your preference.
4. Place a small dollop of kiwi jam in the center of each pastry piece.
5. Fold the pastry over the jam, creating triangles or rectangles, and press the edges to seal.
6. Place the filled pastries on a baking sheet lined with parchment paper.
7. Bake according to the puff pastry package instructions or until the pastries are golden brown and puffed.

8. Allow the pastries to cool slightly before dusting with powdered sugar, if desired.

Recipes for Kiwi-filled Treats:

- Kiwi Jam Danish: Spread kiwi jam on a rolled-out sheet of puff pastry, top with cream cheese, and bake until golden.
- Kiwi Jam Tartlets: Fill tartlet shells with kiwi jam and top with fresh berries for a colorful and delightful dessert.

These special occasion kiwi jam creations add a touch of sophistication to your celebrations and turn everyday pastries into exquisite treats. Enjoy these elegant delights with family and friends!

Chapter 5: Healthier Kiwi Jam Options

5.1 Sugar-Free Kiwi Jam
Catering to Dietary Preferences with a Sugar-Free Alternative
Ingredients:

- 4 cups peeled and diced ripe kiwis
- 1 cup unsweetened apple juice
- 1/4 cup lemon juice
- 1 package (1.75 oz) no-sugar-needed fruit pectin

Instructions:

1. In a large pot, combine the diced kiwis, unsweetened apple juice, and lemon juice. Stir in the no-sugar-needed fruit pectin until well mixed.
2. Place the pot over medium-high heat and bring the kiwi mixture to a full boil, stirring frequently.
3. Once boiling, continue stirring and let the mixture cook for 1-2 minutes.
4. Test the jam's consistency by placing a small amount on a cold plate. If it wrinkles and holds its shape when touched, it's ready.
5. Remove the pot from heat.
6. Ladle the hot jam into sterilized jars, leaving about 1/4-inch headspace. Wipe the jar rims, place sterilized lids, and screw on the bands until fingertip-tight.
7. Process the jars in a boiling water bath for 10 minutes to ensure proper sealing.
8. Allow the jars to cool completely before checking the seals. Store in a cool, dark place.

Natural Sweeteners and Their Impact on Flavor:

- Apple Juice: Adds natural sweetness without the need for refined sugar. Choose unsweetened apple juice for a healthier option.
- Lemon Juice: Enhances the tartness of the kiwis and provides a bright flavor.

5.2 Chia Seed Kiwi Jam
Adding Nutritional Benefits to Your Jams
Ingredients:

- 3 cups peeled and diced ripe kiwis
- 1/4 cup honey or maple syrup (adjust to taste)
- 1/4 cup chia seeds
- 1/4 cup lemon juice

Balancing Texture with Chia Seeds:
Chia seeds absorb liquid and swell, creating a gel-like texture that thickens the jam naturally.
Instructions:

1. In a blender or food processor, pulse the diced kiwis until a chunky puree is formed.
2. Transfer the puree to a bowl and stir in the honey or maple syrup, chia seeds, and lemon juice.
3. Let the mixture sit for 15-20 minutes to allow the chia seeds to absorb liquid and thicken the jam.
4. Taste and adjust the sweetness if necessary.
5. Ladle the chia seed kiwi jam into sterilized jars, leaving about 1/4-inch headspace. Wipe the jar rims, place sterilized lids, and screw on the bands until fingertip-tight.
6. Refrigerate the jars, and the jam will continue to thicken as it cools.

Tips for Chia Seed Kiwi Jam:

- Experiment with the honey or maple syrup quantity to achieve your preferred level of sweetness.
- Stir the jam occasionally during the resting period to ensure even chia seed distribution.

These healthier kiwi jam options provide delicious alternatives for those with dietary preferences, offering the same burst of kiwi flavor with reduced sugar content and added nutritional benefits. Enjoy guilt-free spreads on your favorite dishes!

Chapter 6: Preserving and Storing Kiwi Jams

6.1 Proper Canning Techniques
Step-by-Step Guide to Canning Kiwi Jams
Materials Needed:

- Prepared kiwi jam (hot and freshly made)
- Sterilized canning jars with lids and bands
- Boiling water canner or large pot with a rack
- Jar lifter
- Canning funnel
- Clean cloth or paper towel
- Kitchen timer

Instructions:

1. Prepare Your Jars: Ensure jars are clean and sterilized. Keep them warm until ready to use.
2. Fill the Jars: Using a canning funnel, ladle the hot kiwi jam into the sterilized jars, leaving about 1/4-inch headspace.
3. Remove Air Bubbles: Run a clean spatula or bubble remover tool around the inside edge of the jar to release any trapped air bubbles.
4. Wipe Jar Rims: Use a clean, damp cloth or paper towel to wipe the rims of the jars to ensure a clean seal.
5. Apply Lids and Bands: Place sterilized lids on top of each jar, and screw on the bands until fingertip-tight. Do not overtighten.
6. Process in Boiling Water Bath: Using a jar lifter, carefully place the filled jars into the boiling water canner or a large pot with a rack. Ensure the jars are covered with at least 1-2 inches of

water. Bring water to a rolling boil.

7. Set Timer for Processing: Process the jars in the boiling water bath for 10 minutes, adjusting for altitude if necessary.

8. Remove Jars and Cool: After processing, use the jar lifter to carefully remove the jars from the water bath. Place them on a clean, dry towel or cooling rack to cool completely.

9. Check Seals: Once cooled, press down on the center of each lid. If it doesn't pop back, the jar is sealed.

10. Store Properly: Label the sealed jars with the date and store them in a cool, dark place. Properly sealed jars can be stored for up to a year.

Ensuring Long Shelf Life:

- Check for proper seals before storing. If a jar doesn't seal, refrigerate and use it within a few weeks.
- Store jars away from direct sunlight and extreme temperatures.

6.2 Creative Packaging Ideas
Making Your Kiwi Jams Gift-Worthy
DIY Labels and Packaging Tips:

Custom Labels: Create personalized labels with the name of the jam, ingredients, and a date. Include a special message or recipe suggestion.

Decorative Jars: Use unique or vintage jars to add a touch of charm. Tie a ribbon or twine around the lid for a rustic look.

Gift Baskets: Arrange jars in a gift basket with complementary items, such as crackers, cheeses, or a handwritten recipe card.

Fabric Jar Toppers: Cut circles of fabric and secure them over the jar lids with a rubber band or decorative string.

Embellishments: Add small tags, charms, or dried flowers for an extra touch.

By preserving your kiwi jams using proper canning techniques and creatively packaging them, you can share the delightful flavors with friends and family or create beautiful homemade gifts for any occasion. Enjoy the fruits of your labor and the joy of giving!

Chapter 7: Exotic Kiwi Jam Combinations

7.1 Kiwi Coconut Fusion Jam
A Tropical Twist with the Combination of Kiwi and Coconut
Ingredients:

- 3 cups peeled and diced ripe kiwis
- 1 cup shredded coconut (unsweetened)
- 3 cups granulated sugar
- 1/4 cup lime juice
- 1 package (1.75 oz) fruit pectin

Instructions:

1. In a large pot, combine the diced kiwis, shredded coconut, lime juice, and fruit pectin. Stir well.
2. Place the pot over medium-high heat and bring the mixture to a full boil, stirring frequently.
3. Once boiling, add the granulated sugar all at once, stirring continuously. Return the mixture to a rapid boil and let it boil for 1-2 minutes until the sugar is fully dissolved.
4. Test the jam's consistency by placing a small amount on a cold plate. If it wrinkles and holds its shape when touched, it's ready.
5. Remove the pot from heat and skim off any foam from the surface.
6. Ladle the hot jam into sterilized jars, leaving about 1/4-inch headspace. Wipe the jar rims, place sterilized lids, and screw on the bands until fingertip-tight.
7. Process the jars in a boiling water bath for 10 minutes to ensure proper sealing.
8. Allow the jars to cool completely before checking the seals. Store in a cool, dark place.

Ideal for Summer Spreads and Tropical-Themed Gatherings:

- Spread on toast or muffins for a taste of the tropics at breakfast.
- Use as a topping for tropical fruit salads or ice cream.
- Pair with grilled shrimp or chicken for a sweet and savory glaze.

7.2 Kiwi Mint Infusion Jam
Refreshing Flavors with the Addition of Mint
Ingredients:

- 3 cups peeled and diced ripe kiwis
- 1/4 cup fresh mint leaves, finely chopped
- 3 cups granulated sugar
- 1/4 cup lemon juice
- 1 package (1.75 oz) fruit pectin

Instructions:

1. In a large pot, combine the diced kiwis, chopped mint leaves, lemon juice, and fruit pectin. Stir well.
2. Place the pot over medium-high heat and bring the mixture to a full boil, stirring frequently.
3. Once boiling, add the granulated sugar all at once, stirring continuously. Return the mixture to a rapid boil and let it boil for 1-2 minutes until the sugar is fully dissolved.
4. Test the jam's consistency by placing a small amount on a cold plate. If it wrinkles and holds its shape when touched, it's ready.
5. Remove the pot from heat and skim off any foam from the surface.
6. Ladle the hot jam into sterilized jars, leaving about 1/4-inch headspace. Wipe the jar rims, place sterilized lids, and screw on the bands until fingertip-tight.
7. Process the jars in a boiling water bath for 10 minutes to ensure proper sealing.

8. Allow the jars to cool completely before checking the seals. Store in a cool, dark place.

Perfect for Pairing with Desserts or as a Unique Spread for Appetizers:

- Mix into yogurt or use as a topping for vanilla ice cream.
- Spread on chocolate desserts for a delightful minty kick.
- Pair with goat cheese on crostini for a sophisticated appetizer.

These exotic kiwi jam combinations offer a delightful fusion of flavors, adding a tropical or refreshing twist to your jam repertoire. Explore these unique combinations and let your taste buds embark on a delicious journey!

Chapter 8: Kiwi Jam Marinades and Glazes

8.1 Grilled Kiwi Jam Chicken
Transforming Kiwi Jam into a Flavorful Marinade
Ingredients:

- 4 boneless, skinless chicken breasts
- 1 cup kiwi jam (homemade or store-bought)
- 1/4 cup soy sauce
- 2 tablespoons olive oil
- 2 cloves garlic, minced
- 1 teaspoon ginger, grated
- Salt and pepper to taste
- Fresh cilantro for garnish (optional)

Instructions:

1. In a bowl, whisk together kiwi jam, soy sauce, olive oil, minced garlic, grated ginger, salt, and pepper to create the marinade.
2. Place chicken breasts in a resealable plastic bag or shallow dish and pour half of the marinade over them. Reserve the remaining marinade for basting.
3. Seal the bag or cover the dish and refrigerate for at least 30 minutes, allowing the flavors to infuse.
4. Preheat the grill to medium-high heat.
5. Remove the chicken from the marinade and grill for 6-8 minutes per side or until fully cooked, basting with the reserved marinade.
6. Garnish with fresh cilantro if desired and serve.

Tips for Grilling Perfection:

- Ensure the grill is well preheated before adding the chicken.
- Brush the grill grates with oil to prevent sticking.
- Baste the chicken with the reserved marinade during the last few minutes of grilling for added flavor.

8.2 Kiwi Balsamic Glaze

Elevating Savory Dishes with a Sweet and Tangy Kiwi-Infused Glaze

Ingredients:

- 1 cup kiwi jam (homemade or store-bought)
- 1/2 cup balsamic vinegar
- 2 tablespoons honey
- 1 teaspoon Dijon mustard
- Salt and pepper to taste

Instructions:

1. In a small saucepan, combine kiwi jam, balsamic vinegar, honey, Dijon mustard, salt, and pepper.
2. Bring the mixture to a simmer over medium heat, stirring constantly.
3. Reduce the heat to low and let it simmer for 10-15 minutes or until the glaze thickens.
4. Remove from heat and let it cool slightly before using.
5. Drizzle the kiwi balsamic glaze over grilled meats, roasted vegetables, or use it as a dipping sauce.

Versatile Applications for Meats and Vegetables:

- Brush on grilled pork chops or salmon during the last few minutes of cooking.
- Toss roasted Brussels sprouts or carrots in the glaze before serving.

- Use as a finishing touch for caprese salads or fresh fruit platters.

These kiwi jam marinades and glazes add a burst of flavor to your savory dishes, turning ordinary meals into extraordinary culinary experiences. Enjoy the sweet and tangy infusion of kiwi in your favorite recipes!

Chapter 9: Kiwi Jam Cocktails and Mocktails

9.1 Kiwi Basil Mojito
Crafting Refreshing Beverages with Kiwi Jam
Ingredients:

- 2 tablespoons kiwi jam (homemade or store-bought)
- 8-10 fresh basil leaves
- 1 tablespoon sugar (adjust to taste)
- 1 lime, cut into wedges
- 2 ounces white rum (optional for alcoholic version)
- Club soda
- Ice cubes
- Kiwi slices and basil leaves for garnish

Instructions:

1. In a glass, muddle kiwi jam, basil leaves, sugar, and lime wedges together.
2. Add ice cubes to the glass.
3. Pour rum (if using) over the muddled mixture and stir well.
4. Top with club soda and gently stir again.
5. Garnish with kiwi slices and fresh basil leaves.
6. Serve immediately and enjoy the refreshing Kiwi Basil Mojito!

Non-Alcoholic Variations for All Audiences:

- Omit the rum for a delightful kiwi basil mocktail.
- Substitute sparkling water for club soda to maintain the effervescence without the alcohol.

9.2 Kiwi Jam Bellini

Celebratory Drinks Featuring the Vibrant Flavors of Kiwi

Ingredients:

- 2 tablespoons kiwi jam (homemade or store-bought)
- 1 bottle of chilled prosecco or sparkling water (for mocktail version)
- Fresh mint leaves for garnish
- Kiwi slices for garnish

Instructions:

1. Spoon kiwi jam into the bottom of champagne flutes.
2. Slowly pour chilled prosecco over the kiwi jam, allowing it to mix naturally.
3. Gently stir with a long spoon to enhance the infusion.
4. Garnish with fresh mint leaves and kiwi slices.
5. Serve immediately to enjoy the bubbly Kiwi Jam Bellini.

Serving Suggestions for Brunch or Special Occasions:

- Pair with a brunch spread featuring pastries, fruits, and cheeses.
- Serve at bridal showers, weddings, or other celebratory gatherings for a unique and vibrant drink option.

These kiwi jam cocktails and mocktails offer a delightful way to enjoy the vibrant flavors of kiwi in a refreshing beverage. Whether you're looking for a relaxing mocktail or a spirited cocktail, these recipes cater to all preferences. Cheers to the fusion of kiwi and creative mixology!

Chapter 10: Kiwi Jam Dessert Pairings

10.1 Kiwi Jam Cheesecake
Creating a Decadent Dessert with a Fruity Twist
Ingredients:
For the Crust:

- 1 1/2 cups graham cracker crumbs
- 1/4 cup unsalted butter, melted
- 2 tablespoons sugar

For the Cheesecake Filling:

- 4 packages (32 oz total) cream cheese, softened
- 1 1/4 cups granulated sugar
- 1 teaspoon vanilla extract
- 4 large eggs
- 1 cup kiwi jam (homemade or store-bought)

Instructions:
For the Crust:

1. Preheat the oven to 325°F (163°C). Grease a 9-inch springform pan.
2. In a bowl, combine graham cracker crumbs, melted butter, and sugar. Press the mixture into the bottom of the prepared pan.
3. Bake the crust for 10 minutes, then let it cool while preparing the filling.

For the Cheesecake Filling:

1. In a large mixing bowl, beat the cream cheese, sugar, and vanilla extract until smooth and creamy.
2. Add the eggs one at a time, beating well after each addition.

3. Pour the cream cheese filling over the cooled crust.

4. Spoon dollops of kiwi jam over the cream cheese filling. Use a knife to gently swirl the jam into the batter for a marbled effect.

5. Bake for 55-60 minutes or until the center is set and the top is lightly browned.

6. Allow the cheesecake to cool completely in the pan before refrigerating for at least 4 hours or overnight.

7. Run a knife around the edge of the pan before releasing the springform sides.

8. Slice and serve the Kiwi Jam Cheesecake.

Tips for Achieving the Perfect Cheesecake Texture:

- Use room temperature cream cheese to ensure a smooth batter.
- Avoid overmixing the batter once the eggs are added to prevent cracking during baking.
- Allow the cheesecake to cool gradually to prevent cracks.

10.2 Kiwi Jam Ice Cream Topping

Elevating Your Favorite Ice Cream Flavors with a Spoonful of Kiwi Goodness

Ingredients:

- Vanilla ice cream (or your favorite flavor)
- Kiwi jam (homemade or store-bought)
- Sliced kiwi for garnish
- Chopped nuts (optional)

DIY Ice Cream Sundae Ideas:

- Classic Kiwi Sundae: Scoop vanilla ice cream into a bowl, drizzle with kiwi jam, and top with sliced kiwi.
- Tropical Delight: Use coconut or pineapple-flavored ice cream, add kiwi jam, and garnish with sliced kiwi for a tropical twist.

- Nutty Kiwi Explosion: Sprinkle chopped nuts over vanilla ice cream, generously spoon kiwi jam, and top with sliced kiwi.
- Kiwi Chocolate Indulgence: Pair chocolate ice cream with kiwi jam for a unique and indulgent flavor combination.

Add a spoonful of kiwi jam to your ice cream for a burst of fruity sweetness that enhances your favorite frozen treats. Enjoy these dessert pairings that showcase the versatility of kiwi in delightful ways!

Chapter 11: International Kiwi Jam Inspirations

11.1 Kiwi Mango Tango Jam (Tropical Fusion)
Exploring Global Fruit Combinations with Kiwi
Ingredients:

- 3 cups peeled and diced ripe kiwis
- 2 cups peeled, pitted, and diced mangoes
- 3 cups granulated sugar
- 1/4 cup lime juice
- 1 package (1.75 oz) fruit pectin

Instructions:

1. In a large pot, combine diced kiwis, diced mangoes, lime juice, and fruit pectin. Stir well.
2. Place the pot over medium-high heat and bring the mixture to a full boil, stirring frequently.
3. Once boiling, add granulated sugar all at once, stirring continuously. Return the mixture to a rapid boil and let it boil for 1-2 minutes until the sugar is fully dissolved.
4. Test the jam's consistency by placing a small amount on a cold plate. If it wrinkles and holds its shape when touched, it's ready.
5. Remove the pot from heat and skim off any foam from the surface.
6. Ladle the hot jam into sterilized jars, leaving about 1/4-inch headspace. Wipe the jar rims, place sterilized lids, and screw on the bands until fingertip-tight.
7. Process the jars in a boiling water bath for 10 minutes to ensure proper sealing.
8. Allow the jars to cool completely before checking the seals.

Store in a cool, dark place.

Fusion Jams Inspired by Different Cuisines:

- Caribbean Twist: Add a splash of rum during the cooking process for a tropical Caribbean flair.
- Mediterranean Fusion: Infuse the jam with a hint of basil or mint for a refreshing twist inspired by Mediterranean cuisine.

11.2 Kiwi Lychee Harmony Jam (Asian Fusion)
Infusing Kiwi with Asian Flavors for a Unique Jam Experience
Ingredients:

- 3 cups peeled and diced ripe kiwis
- 1 cup peeled and diced lychees
- 3 cups granulated sugar
- 1/4 cup lemon juice
- 1 package (1.75 oz) fruit pectin

Recipe Variations with Lychee and Other Exotic Fruits:

- Tropical Paradise: Include diced pineapple and passion fruit for an extra tropical burst.
- Citrus Infusion: Enhance the Asian fusion experience by adding a touch of grated ginger and orange zest.

Instructions:

1. In a large pot, combine diced kiwis, diced lychees, lemon juice, and fruit pectin. Stir well.
2. Place the pot over medium-high heat and bring the mixture to a full boil, stirring frequently.
3. Once boiling, add granulated sugar all at once, stirring

continuously. Return the mixture to a rapid boil and let it boil for 1-2 minutes until the sugar is fully dissolved.

4. Test the jam's consistency by placing a small amount on a cold plate. If it wrinkles and holds its shape when touched, it's ready.

5. Remove the pot from heat and skim off any foam from the surface.

6. Ladle the hot jam into sterilized jars, leaving about 1/4-inch headspace. Wipe the jar rims, place sterilized lids, and screw on the bands until fingertip-tight.

7. Process the jars in a boiling water bath for 10 minutes to ensure proper sealing.

8. Allow the jars to cool completely before checking the seals. Store in a cool, dark place.

These international kiwi jam inspirations showcase the versatility of kiwi in combining with fruits from around the world. Experiment with different flavor profiles to create unique fusion jams inspired by diverse cuisines!

Chapter 12: Kiwi Jam for Breakfast

12.1 Kiwi Jam Pancake Syrup
A Sweet Topping for Your Morning Pancakes or Waffles
Ingredients:

- 1 cup kiwi jam (homemade or store-bought)
- 1/4 cup maple syrup
- 1 tablespoon lemon juice

Instructions:

1. In a small saucepan, combine kiwi jam, maple syrup, and lemon juice.
2. Heat the mixture over medium heat, stirring frequently.
3. Once the mixture is heated through, remove from heat and let it cool slightly.
4. Pour the Kiwi Jam Pancake Syrup over your favorite pancakes or waffles.
5. Enjoy the delightful fusion of kiwi sweetness and maple goodness!

Breakfast Recipes Featuring Kiwi Jam:

- Kiwi Jam Stuffed French Toast: Make a sandwich with two slices of bread and a layer of kiwi jam. Dip in a mixture of eggs and milk, then cook until golden brown.
- Kiwi Jam Breakfast Burrito: Spread kiwi jam on a tortilla, add yogurt, granola, and sliced bananas. Roll it up for a delicious breakfast on the go.

12.2 Kiwi Jam Yogurt Parfait
Creating a Healthy and Flavorful Yogurt Parfait with Kiwi Jam

Ingredients:

- Greek yogurt (or your favorite yogurt)
- Kiwi jam (homemade or store-bought)
- Granola
- Fresh berries (e.g., strawberries, blueberries)
- Honey for drizzling
- Mint leaves for garnish

Layering Tips for a Visually Appealing Presentation:

- Bottom Layer: Spoon a layer of Greek yogurt into the bottom of a glass or bowl.
- Middle Layer: Add a dollop of kiwi jam over the yogurt.
- Next Layer: Sprinkle granola for crunch and texture.
- Top Layer: Add another layer of yogurt.
- Final Touch: Top with fresh berries, drizzle with honey, and garnish with mint leaves.

Variations:

Tropical Paradise Parfait: Include diced tropical fruits like mango and pineapple.

Nutty Kiwi Crunch: Add a layer of chopped nuts for extra crunch.

This breakfast chapter introduces delightful ways to incorporate kiwi jam into your morning routine. From a sweet pancake syrup to a healthy and visually appealing yogurt parfait, these recipes bring the vibrant flavor of kiwi to the breakfast table!

Chapter 13: Quick and Easy Kiwi Jam Snacks

13.1 Kiwi Jam Granola Bars

Adding a Burst of Flavor to Homemade Granola Bars

Ingredients:

- 2 cups old-fashioned oats
- 1 cup crispy rice cereal
- 1/2 cup chopped nuts (e.g., almonds, walnuts)
- 1/2 cup honey or maple syrup
- 1/2 cup almond butter or peanut butter
- 1/2 cup kiwi jam (homemade or store-bought)
- 1 teaspoon vanilla extract
- A pinch of salt

Instructions:

1. In a large mixing bowl, combine oats, crispy rice cereal, and chopped nuts.
2. In a saucepan over medium heat, warm honey (or maple syrup) and almond butter (or peanut butter), stirring until melted and well combined.
3. Remove the saucepan from heat and stir in kiwi jam and vanilla extract.
4. Pour the wet mixture over the dry ingredients and mix thoroughly to coat.
5. Press the mixture into a lined baking dish and refrigerate for at least 2 hours to set.
6. Once set, cut into bars and enjoy these Kiwi Jam Granola Bars as quick and flavorful snacks.

Perfect for On-the-Go Snacks:

- Wrap individually for a convenient snack during busy days.
- Pair with a piece of fruit for a balanced on-the-go snack.

13.2 Kiwi Jam Stuffed Pretzels
Savory and Sweet Combination with a Kiwi Jam Filling
Ingredients:

- Soft pretzels (store-bought or homemade)
- Kiwi jam (homemade or store-bought)
- Powdered sugar for dusting (optional)

Instructions:

1. Preheat the oven according to the pretzel package instructions if using store-bought.
2. Take each soft pretzel and create a small pocket in the center by gently tearing it open.
3. Spoon a dollop of kiwi jam into the pocket of each pretzel.
4. Close the pretzel, ensuring the jam is sealed inside.
5. Bake the pretzels according to package instructions or until they achieve a golden-brown color.
6. Once baked, dust with powdered sugar if desired.
7. Serve warm and enjoy these Kiwi Jam Stuffed Pretzels for a delightful snack.

Ideal for Parties or Casual Gatherings:

- Arrange on a platter for a sweet and savory appetizer.
- Serve as a unique addition to a snack board or grazing table.

These quick and easy kiwi jam snacks provide a burst of flavor in convenient and portable forms. From energy-packed granola bars to the delightful combination of sweet kiwi jam inside soft pretzels, these snacks are perfect for satisfying cravings on the go or impressing guests at gatherings.

Chapter 14: Kiwi Jam Salad Dressings

14.1 Kiwi Poppy Seed Vinaigrette
Enhancing Salads with a Fruity and Tangy Dressing
Ingredients:

- 1/2 cup olive oil
- 1/4 cup kiwi jam (homemade or store-bought)
- 2 tablespoons white wine vinegar
- 1 tablespoon Dijon mustard
- 1 tablespoon honey
- 1 teaspoon poppy seeds
- Salt and pepper to taste

Instructions:

1. In a bowl, whisk together olive oil, kiwi jam, white wine vinegar, Dijon mustard, honey, poppy seeds, salt, and pepper until well combined.
2. Taste and adjust the sweetness or acidity according to your preference.
3. Drizzle the Kiwi Poppy Seed Vinaigrette over your favorite salads just before serving.

Pairing Suggestions for Different Types of Salads:

- Fruit Salad: Toss with a mix of fresh fruits, nuts, and greens.
- Chicken Salad: Drizzle over a grilled chicken salad with mixed greens and cherry tomatoes.
- Spinach Salad: Pair with baby spinach, feta cheese, and candied walnuts.

14.2 Kiwi Honey Mustard Glaze

A Sweet and Savory Dressing for Grilled Meats and Salads
Ingredients:

- 1/4 cup kiwi jam (homemade or store-bought)
- 2 tablespoons Dijon mustard
- 2 tablespoons honey
- 1 tablespoon soy sauce
- 1 clove garlic, minced
- Salt and pepper to taste

Instructions:

1. In a small bowl, whisk together kiwi jam, Dijon mustard, honey, soy sauce, minced garlic, salt, and pepper until well combined.
2. Taste and adjust the sweetness or saltiness according to your preference.
3. Use the Kiwi Honey Mustard Glaze as a dressing for grilled meats or a flavorful addition to salads.

Balancing Flavors for the Perfect Glaze:

- Grilled Chicken Glaze: Brush over chicken breasts or thighs during grilling for a sweet and savory coating.
- Vegetable Glaze: Toss roasted vegetables in the glaze before serving for added flavor.
- Quinoa Salad Dressing: Mix with cooked quinoa, diced vegetables, and herbs for a refreshing side dish.

These kiwi jam salad dressings add a burst of flavor to your salads and grilled dishes, enhancing your dining experience with a fruity and tangy twist. Experiment with different pairings to discover the perfect combination for your taste preferences.

Chapter 15: Kiwi Jam Holiday Specialties

15.1 Kiwi Cranberry Relish

A Festive Twist on Traditional Cranberry Sauce

Ingredients:

- 1 cup fresh or frozen cranberries
- 1 cup kiwi jam (homemade or store-bought)
- 1/2 cup granulated sugar
- 1/4 cup orange juice
- 1 teaspoon orange zest

Instructions:

1. In a saucepan, combine cranberries, kiwi jam, granulated sugar, orange juice, and orange zest.
2. Bring the mixture to a boil over medium-high heat, stirring occasionally.
3. Reduce the heat to low and simmer for 10-15 minutes, or until the cranberries burst and the sauce thickens.
4. Remove from heat and let it cool before serving.
5. Refrigerate until ready to use.

Perfect for Thanksgiving and Holiday Feasts:

Serve alongside turkey or ham for a unique and flavorful cranberry relish.

Spread on sandwiches or use as a topping for holiday appetizers.

15.2 Kiwi Jam Christmas Cookies

Incorporating Kiwi Jam into Holiday Cookie Recipes

Ingredients:

- 1 cup unsalted butter, softened
- 3/4 cup granulated sugar

- 1 large egg
- 2 teaspoons vanilla extract
- 2 1/2 cups all-purpose flour
- 1/2 teaspoon baking powder
- 1/4 teaspoon salt
- Kiwi jam (homemade or store-bought)
- Powdered sugar for dusting (optional)

Instructions:

1. In a large bowl, cream together softened butter and granulated sugar until light and fluffy.
2. Beat in the egg and vanilla extract until well combined.
3. In a separate bowl, whisk together flour, baking powder, and salt.
4. Gradually add the dry ingredients to the wet ingredients, mixing until the dough comes together.
5. Divide the dough into two equal portions, shape each into a disc, wrap in plastic wrap, and refrigerate for at least 1 hour.
6. Preheat the oven to 350°F (175°C) and line baking sheets with parchment paper.
7. Roll out one disc of dough on a floured surface and cut out desired shapes using holiday-themed cookie cutters.
8. Place cookies on the prepared baking sheets and make a small indentation in the center of each cookie using your thumb or the back of a spoon.
9. Spoon a small amount of kiwi jam into each indentation.
10. Roll out the second disc of dough and cut out shapes to place on top of the jam-filled cookies, creating a sandwich.
11. Press the edges to seal and bake for 10-12 minutes or until the edges are lightly golden.
12. Allow the cookies to cool on the baking sheets for a few minutes before transferring them to a wire rack to cool completely.

13. Dust with powdered sugar if desired.

Festive Cookie Decorating Ideas:

- Use colored icing to create holiday patterns or designs on the cookies.
- Sprinkle edible glitter or colored sugar for a festive touch.

These Kiwi Jam Holiday Specialties bring a unique and flavorful twist to your festive celebrations. Whether you're looking for a delightful cranberry relish or a creative way to incorporate kiwi jam into your Christmas cookies, these recipes are sure to add a burst of holiday cheer to your table!

Chapter 16: Kiwi Jam for Entertaining

16.1 Kiwi Jam Charcuterie Board

Elevating Your Charcuterie Spread with Sweet and Savory Kiwi Jams

Pairing Suggestions for Cheeses, Meats, and Accompaniments:

Cheeses:

Brie: Pair with Kiwi Champagne Jam for an elegant combination.

Blue Cheese: Complement with Spicy Kiwi Jalapeño Jam for a sweet and spicy contrast.

Goat Cheese: Enhance with Kiwi Berry Bliss Jam for a fruity and tangy profile.

Aged Cheddar: Pair with Classic Kiwi Jam for a simple and delicious match.

Meats:

Prosciutto: Wrap around melon slices and top with Kiwi Lime Fusion Jam.

Salami: Serve with slices of Kiwi Mango Tango Jam for a tropical twist.

Soppressata: Pair with Kiwi Coconut Fusion Jam for a unique flavor experience.

Smoked Salmon: Spread Creamy Kiwi Chia Seed Jam on crackers and top with smoked salmon.

Accompaniments:

Crackers and Bread: Offer a variety of crackers and bread to complement the cheese and jam pairings.

Nuts: Include a mix of nuts like almonds, walnuts, and pistachios for added crunch.

Dried Fruits: Add sweetness with dried apricots, figs, or raisins.

Fresh Fruits: Include slices of apple, pear, and grapes for a refreshing contrast.

16.2 Kiwi Jam Cocktail Hour Bites

Creating Delectable Appetizers Using Kiwi Jam as a Key Ingredient

Appetizer Ideas:
1. Kiwi Jam & Brie Crostini:

- Baguette slices toasted until golden.
- Spread a layer of Kiwi Mango Tango Jam on each slice.
- Top with a slice of brie cheese and a sprinkle of chopped pistachios.

2. Kiwi Jam Meatballs:

- Make meatballs using your favorite ground meat (e.g., beef, turkey, or chicken).
- Coat the meatballs in a glaze made from a mixture of kiwi jam, soy sauce, and a touch of ginger.
- Bake until cooked through and glazed.

3. Kiwi Jam Bruschetta:

- Combine diced tomatoes, red onion, fresh basil, and Kiwi Berry Bliss Jam.
- Spoon the mixture onto toasted baguette slices.
- Optional: Top with crumbled feta or goat cheese.

4. Kiwi Jam and Cream Cheese Stuffed Peppers:

- Cut mini bell peppers in half and remove seeds.
- Fill each half with a mixture of cream cheese and Kiwi Lime Fusion Jam.
- Sprinkle with chopped chives for garnish.

5. Kiwi Jam Shrimp Skewers:

- Marinate shrimp in a mixture of kiwi jam, garlic, and lime juice.

- Thread onto skewers and grill until cooked.
- Serve with an extra drizzle of kiwi jam glaze.

These Kiwi Jam Entertaining ideas provide a delightful array of sweet and savory options to impress your guests. From a carefully curated charcuterie board to delectable cocktail hour bites, these recipes are perfect for elevating your entertaining experience at cocktail parties and social gatherings.

Chapter 17: Kiwi Jam Chutneys and Salsas

17.1 Spiced Kiwi Chutney

Adding a Touch of Spice and Complexity to Your Jams

Ingredients:

- 2 cups peeled and diced ripe kiwis
- 1 cup brown sugar
- 1 cup white vinegar
- 1 small onion, finely chopped
- 1/2 cup raisins
- 1 teaspoon ground ginger
- 1 teaspoon mustard seeds
- 1/2 teaspoon ground cinnamon
- 1/4 teaspoon ground cloves
- 1/4 teaspoon red pepper flakes (adjust to taste)
- Salt to taste

Instructions:

1. In a large saucepan, combine diced kiwis, brown sugar, white vinegar, chopped onion, raisins, ground ginger, mustard seeds, ground cinnamon, ground cloves, red pepper flakes, and salt.
2. Bring the mixture to a boil over medium-high heat, stirring frequently.
3. Reduce the heat to low and simmer for 30-40 minutes, or until the chutney thickens and the flavors meld together.
4. Remove from heat and let it cool before transferring to sterilized jars.
5. Refrigerate until ready to use.

Pairing Ideas with Grilled Meats and Indian Cuisine:

Grilled Chicken: Serve Spiced Kiwi Chutney as a flavorful topping for grilled chicken.

Indian Dishes: Use as a condiment alongside traditional Indian dishes such as samosas or curry.

17.2 Kiwi Mango Salsa

A Tropical Salsa Featuring the Vibrant Flavors of Kiwi and Mango

Ingredients:

- 2 cups peeled and diced ripe kiwis
- 1 cup peeled, pitted, and diced mangoes
- 1/2 cup diced red onion
- 1/4 cup chopped fresh cilantro
- 1 jalapeño, seeds removed and finely chopped
- Juice of 2 limes
- Salt to taste

Instructions:

1. In a bowl, combine diced kiwis, diced mangoes, diced red onion, chopped cilantro, chopped jalapeño, lime juice, and salt.
2. Toss the ingredients together until well mixed.
3. Refrigerate the Kiwi Mango Salsa for at least 30 minutes before serving to allow the flavors to meld.

Serving Suggestions for Tacos, Grilled Fish, and More:

Fish Tacos: Top your favorite fish tacos with Kiwi Mango Salsa for a burst of tropical freshness.

Grilled Fish: Serve alongside grilled fish fillets for a vibrant and flavorful topping.

Chicken Salad: Mix into a chicken salad for a fruity and spicy kick.

These Kiwi Jam Chutneys and Salsas offer a delightful fusion of flavors, adding complexity to your dishes. Whether you're spicing up grilled meats with Spiced Kiwi Chutney or bringing a tropical twist to tacos with Kiwi Mango Salsa, these recipes are versatile and sure to impress your taste buds!

Chapter 18: Kiwi Jam in Savory Sauces

18.1 Kiwi Teriyaki Glaze

Incorporating Kiwi Jam into Asian-Inspired Teriyaki Sauces

Ingredients:

- 1 cup soy sauce
- 1/2 cup kiwi jam (homemade or store-bought)
- 1/4 cup rice vinegar
- 3 tablespoons brown sugar
- 2 tablespoons grated ginger
- 2 cloves garlic, minced
- 1 tablespoon cornstarch (optional, for thickening)
- Sesame seeds for garnish (optional)

Instructions:

1. In a saucepan, combine soy sauce, kiwi jam, rice vinegar, brown sugar, grated ginger, and minced garlic.
2. Bring the mixture to a simmer over medium heat, stirring frequently.
3. Optional: If a thicker consistency is desired, mix cornstarch with a little water to create a slurry. Stir the slurry into the sauce and continue simmering until thickened.
4. Remove from heat and let the Kiwi Teriyaki Glaze cool slightly.
5. Brush the glaze over grilled meats, use in stir-fries, or drizzle over rice bowls.
6. Garnish with sesame seeds if desired.

Ideal for Glazing Meats, Stir-Fries, and Rice Bowls:

Grilled Chicken: Brush Kiwi Teriyaki Glaze over grilled chicken for a sweet and tangy finish.

Stir-Fried Vegetables: Toss stir-fried vegetables in the glaze for an Asian-inspired twist.

Teriyaki Rice Bowl: Drizzle over a bowl of teriyaki chicken, rice, and vegetables.

18.2 Creamy Kiwi Dijon Sauce

Balancing Sweetness and Tanginess in a Creamy Dijon Sauce

Ingredients:

- 1/2 cup kiwi jam (homemade or store-bought)
- 1/4 cup Dijon mustard
- 1/4 cup mayonnaise
- 1 tablespoon white wine vinegar
- 1 tablespoon honey
- Salt and pepper to taste

Instructions:

1. In a bowl, whisk together kiwi jam, Dijon mustard, mayonnaise, white wine vinegar, honey, salt, and pepper until well combined.
2. Taste and adjust the sweetness or tanginess according to your preference.
3. Refrigerate the Creamy Kiwi Dijon Sauce until ready to use.

Pairing Suggestions for Chicken, Pork, and Vegetables:

Grilled Pork Chops: Serve alongside grilled pork chops for a flavorful accompaniment.

Chicken Tenders: Dip chicken tenders into the sauce for a tasty appetizer.

Roasted Vegetables: Toss roasted vegetables in the sauce before serving.

These savory sauce recipes showcase the versatility of kiwi jam in creating flavorful glazes and condiments. Whether you're adding a sweet and tangy kick to teriyaki dishes or balancing sweetness and tanginess in a creamy Dijon sauce, these recipes are sure to enhance your savory culinary creations!

Chapter 19: Kiwi Jam Baked Goods

19.1 Kiwi Jam-Filled Muffins

Creating Moist and Flavorful Muffins with a Surprise Kiwi Jam Center

Ingredients:

- 2 cups all-purpose flour
- 1 cup granulated sugar
- 1 teaspoon baking powder
- 1/2 teaspoon baking soda
- 1/4 teaspoon salt
- 1/2 cup unsalted butter, melted
- 2 large eggs
- 1 cup buttermilk
- 1 teaspoon vanilla extract
- Kiwi jam (homemade or store-bought)

Instructions:

1. Preheat the oven to 375°F (190°C) and line a muffin tin with paper liners.
2. In a large bowl, whisk together flour, sugar, baking powder, baking soda, and salt.
3. In a separate bowl, whisk together melted butter, eggs, buttermilk, and vanilla extract.
4. Add the wet ingredients to the dry ingredients, stirring until just combined.
5. Fill each muffin cup halfway with batter.
6. Place a small spoonful of kiwi jam in the center of each cup.
7. Top with the remaining batter to cover the jam.
8. Bake for 18-20 minutes or until a toothpick inserted into the

center of a muffin comes out clean.

9. Allow the muffins to cool in the tin for 5 minutes before transferring them to a wire rack to cool completely.

Ideal for Breakfast or as a Snack:

Enjoy the Kiwi Jam-Filled Muffins for a delightful breakfast or a sweet afternoon snack.

Customize with your favorite jam flavors for variety.

19.2 Kiwi Jam Swirl Bread

Adding a Fruity Swirl to Your Homemade Bread

Ingredients:

- 3 cups all-purpose flour
- 1/4 cup granulated sugar
- 1 teaspoon salt
- 1 tablespoon active dry yeast
- 1 cup warm milk
- 2 tablespoons unsalted butter, melted
- 1 large egg
- Kiwi jam (homemade or store-bought)

Instructions:

1. In a bowl, combine warm milk and active dry yeast. Let it sit for 5 minutes until frothy.
2. In a large bowl, whisk together flour, sugar, and salt.
3. Add the yeast mixture, melted butter, and egg to the dry ingredients. Mix until a dough forms.
4. Knead the dough on a floured surface until smooth and elastic.
5. Place the dough in a greased bowl, cover with a damp cloth, and let it rise in a warm place until doubled in size.
6. Punch down the risen dough and roll it out into a rectangle on

a floured surface.

7. Spread a layer of kiwi jam over the surface of the dough.
8. Roll the dough tightly into a log and place it in a greased loaf pan.
9. Cover and let it rise again until it reaches the top of the pan.
10. Preheat the oven to 375°F (190°C) and bake for 25-30 minutes or until the bread is golden brown.
11. Allow the Kiwi Jam Swirl Bread to cool before slicing.

Tips for Achieving the Perfect Swirl Pattern:
Ensure the jam is evenly spread over the rolled-out dough.

Roll the dough tightly to create distinct swirls.

Use a toothpick or skewer to create a marbled effect by gently swirling the jam into the dough.

These Kiwi Jam Baked Goods recipes bring a burst of fruity goodness to your breakfast or snack time. Whether you're biting into a muffin with a surprise kiwi jam center or savoring the delightful swirls in homemade bread, these baked goods are sure to be a hit!

Chapter 20: Kiwi Jam Infused Beverages

20.1 Kiwi Iced Tea Elixir

Crafting a Refreshing Iced Tea Infused with the Essence of Kiwi

Ingredients:

- 4 cups brewed black tea, cooled
- 1/2 cup kiwi jam (homemade or store-bought)
- 1/4 cup honey or to taste
- 1 lemon, sliced
- Ice cubes
- Fresh mint leaves for garnish

Instructions:

1. In a pitcher, combine brewed black tea, kiwi jam, and honey. Stir well until the jam is fully dissolved.
2. Add lemon slices to the mixture for an extra citrusy kick.
3. Refrigerate the Kiwi Iced Tea Elixir for at least 2 hours to allow the flavors to meld.
4. Serve over ice and garnish with fresh mint leaves.

Ideal for Warm Weather or as a Thirst-Quencher:

Enjoy the Kiwi Iced Tea Elixir on a sunny day for a refreshing and hydrating experience.

Customize sweetness by adjusting the amount of honey according to your preference.

20.2 Kiwi Lemonade Spritzer

Sparkling Beverages Featuring the Sweetness of Kiwi Jam

Ingredients:

- 1 cup kiwi jam (homemade or store-bought)
- 1 cup freshly squeezed lemon juice

- 1/2 cup simple syrup (adjust to taste)
- 2 cups sparkling water
- Ice cubes
- Lemon slices and kiwi slices for garnish

Instructions:

1. In a blender, combine kiwi jam, freshly squeezed lemon juice, and simple syrup. Blend until smooth.
2. Strain the mixture to remove any pulp, resulting in a smooth kiwi lemonade base.
3. In a serving pitcher, mix the kiwi lemonade base with sparkling water.
4. Fill glasses with ice cubes and pour the Kiwi Lemonade Spritzer over the ice.
5. Garnish with lemon slices and kiwi slices for a visually appealing presentation.

Perfect for Summer Picnics and Outdoor Gatherings:

Serve the Kiwi Lemonade Spritzer at picnics, barbecues, or any outdoor event for a fizzy and fruity treat.

Experiment with different sparkling water flavors for added variety.

These Kiwi Jam Infused Beverages offer a delightful twist to your favorite summer drinks. Whether you're sipping on a refreshing Kiwi Iced Tea Elixir or enjoying the fizzy goodness of a Kiwi Lemonade Spritzer, these beverages are perfect for staying cool and hydrated during warm weather or as a special treat for outdoor gatherings.

Chapter 21: Kiwi Jam Breakfast Bowls

21.1 Kiwi Jam Acai Bowl
Creating a Vibrant and Nutritious Acai Bowl with Kiwi Jam
Ingredients:

- 2 frozen acai packets
- 1/2 cup frozen mixed berries
- 1 ripe banana
- 1/2 cup almond milk
- 2 tablespoons kiwi jam (homemade or store-bought)
- Toppings: Granola, sliced kiwi, chia seeds, coconut flakes, and a drizzle of additional kiwi jam

Instructions:

- In a blender, combine frozen acai packets, frozen mixed berries, ripe banana, almond milk, and kiwi jam.
- Blend until smooth and creamy, adding more almond milk if needed.
- Pour the acai mixture into a bowl.
- Arrange your desired toppings on the acai bowl, such as granola, sliced kiwi, chia seeds, coconut flakes, and a drizzle of additional kiwi jam.
- Enjoy this vibrant Kiwi Jam Acai Bowl as a nutrient-packed and delicious breakfast.

Toppings and Variations for a Customizable Breakfast:
Fresh Fruits: Add a variety of fresh fruits like berries, banana slices, or mango chunks.

Nuts and Seeds: Sprinkle with your favorite nuts and seeds for added crunch and nutrition.

Nut Butter: Drizzle almond butter or peanut butter for a creamy finish.

21.2 Kiwi Jam Overnight Oats

Preparing a Quick and Delicious Breakfast with the Addition of Kiwi Jam

Ingredients:

- 1/2 cup rolled oats
- 1/2 cup milk (dairy or plant-based)
- 1/2 cup Greek yogurt
- 2 tablespoons kiwi jam (homemade or store-bought)
- 1 tablespoon chia seeds
- 1/2 teaspoon vanilla extract
- Toppings: Sliced kiwi, nuts, and a dollop of kiwi jam

Instructions:

1. In a jar or container, combine rolled oats, milk, Greek yogurt, kiwi jam, chia seeds, and vanilla extract.
2. Stir well to ensure all ingredients are combined.
3. Seal the jar or container and refrigerate overnight or for at least 4 hours.
4. In the morning, give the oats a good stir and add additional milk if desired.
5. Top with sliced kiwi, your favorite nuts, and a dollop of kiwi jam.
6. Enjoy these Kiwi Jam Overnight Oats for a quick and satisfying breakfast.

Ideas for Flavor Combinations and Toppings:

Tropical Twist: Add shredded coconut, pineapple chunks, and passion fruit.

Nutty Delight: Top with chopped almonds, walnuts, or hazelnuts.

Chocolate Indulgence: Mix in cocoa powder and top with chocolate chips.

These Kiwi Jam Breakfast Bowl recipes offer a delightful start to your day, whether you prefer the refreshing goodness of an Acai Bowl or the convenience of Overnight Oats. Customize your bowls with an array of toppings for a breakfast that suits your taste and provides the energy you need.

Chapter 22: Kiwi Jam Fusion Desserts

22.1 Kiwi Tiramisu

Putting a Fruity Twist on the Classic Italian Dessert

Ingredients:

- 1 cup strong brewed coffee, cooled
- 3 tablespoons coffee liqueur (optional)
- 3 large egg yolks
- 1/2 cup granulated sugar
- 1 cup mascarpone cheese
- 1 cup heavy cream
- Ladyfinger cookies
- 2 tablespoons kiwi jam (homemade or store-bought)
- Sliced kiwi for garnish
- Cocoa powder for dusting

Layering Techniques and Flavor Combinations:

1. In a bowl, combine brewed coffee and coffee liqueur. Set aside.
2. In a separate bowl, whisk together egg yolks and sugar until pale and creamy.
3. Add mascarpone cheese to the egg yolk mixture and mix until smooth.
4. In another bowl, whip the heavy cream until stiff peaks form.
5. Gently fold the whipped cream into the mascarpone mixture until well combined.
6. Dip each ladyfinger into the coffee mixture and arrange them in a layer in a serving dish.
7. Spread a layer of the mascarpone mixture over the ladyfingers.
8. Repeat the layers, ending with a mascarpone layer on top.
9. Heat the kiwi jam for a few seconds to make it more spreadable

and swirl it over the top layer.

10. Refrigerate the Kiwi Tiramisu for at least 4 hours or overnight.
11. Before serving, dust the top with cocoa powder and garnish with sliced kiwi.

22.2 Kiwi Chocolate Fondue
Elevating Your Chocolate Fondue Experience with Kiwi Jam
Ingredients:

- 8 ounces dark chocolate, finely chopped
- 1/2 cup heavy cream
- 2 tablespoons kiwi jam (homemade or store-bought)
- Dipping Suggestions: Sliced kiwi, strawberries, banana slices, marshmallows, pretzels, and cubed pound cake

Dipping Suggestions for a Fun and Interactive Dessert:

1. In a heatproof bowl, combine chopped dark chocolate and heavy cream.
2. Place the bowl over a pot of simmering water (double boiler) and stir until the chocolate is melted and smooth.
3. Stir in kiwi jam until well combined.
4. Transfer the chocolate fondue to a serving bowl or fondue pot.
5. Arrange an assortment of dipping suggestions on a platter.
6. Invite guests to dip their favorite treats into the luscious Kiwi Chocolate Fondue.

Enjoy a Fun and Interactive Dessert:
Experiment with different fruits, cookies, and treats for dipping.
Encourage guests to customize their own dessert creations.
These Kiwi Jam Fusion Desserts add a creative and flavorful twist to classic favorites. Whether you're savoring the layers of Kiwi Tiramisu or indulging in the interactive experience of Kiwi Chocolate Fondue, these desserts are sure to be a hit at any gathering or special occasion.

❖ Conclusion:

Explore and Create Your Own Kiwi Jam Variations

As we reach the end of our flavorful journey through "Kiwi Jam Delights," let's recap the key tips and techniques that have guided you in mastering the art of kiwi jam-making. From selecting the ripest kiwis to crafting exquisite jams for various occasions, you've embarked on a culinary adventure that celebrates the sweet, tangy essence of kiwi fruit.

Recap of Key Tips and Techniques:

Choosing the Right Kiwis: Selecting ripe kiwi fruits and understanding the nuances of different kiwi varieties lay the foundation for delicious jams.

Essential Equipment and Ingredients: Equipping your kitchen with the necessary tools and using high-quality ingredients ensure the success of your kiwi jam endeavors.

Basic Kiwi Jam Recipes: Master the classic with the straightforward Classic Kiwi Jam and explore the zesty Kiwi Lime Fusion Jam for a citrusy twist.

Creative Variations: Elevate your jam experience with spicy notes in the Spicy Kiwi Jalapeño Jam or embrace a fruity blend in the Kiwi Berry Bliss Jam.

Special Occasion Creations: Celebrate in style with the sophistication of Kiwi Champagne Jam or indulge in Kiwi Jam-filled Pastries for delightful treats.

Healthier Options: Cater to diverse preferences with Sugar-Free Kiwi Jam and embrace the nutritional benefits of Chia Seed Kiwi Jam.

Preserving and Storing: Ensure the longevity of your creations by mastering proper canning techniques and exploring creative packaging ideas.

International Inspirations: Take a global culinary journey with exotic combinations like Kiwi Mango Tango Jam and Kiwi Lychee Harmony Jam.

Kiwi Jam in Various Dishes: From breakfast delights to beverages, desserts, and savory sauces, discover the versatility of kiwi jams in the kitchen.

Entertaining and Artisanal Pairings: Impress guests with Kiwi Jam Cheese Plates, wine pairings, and explore the world of artisanal combinations.

Kiwi Jam Fusion Desserts: Indulge in the fruity twist of Kiwi Tiramisu and elevate your chocolate fondue experience with Kiwi Chocolate Fondue.

Encouragement to Explore and Create:

As you conclude this journey, let the spirit of creativity and exploration continue to guide you. Don't be afraid to experiment with new flavor combinations, tweak recipes to suit your taste, and create your signature kiwi jam variations. The beauty of jam-making lies in the endless possibilities and the joy of sharing your creations with loved ones.

So, set forth with newfound knowledge, armed with the skills to craft exquisite kiwi jams and the confidence to infuse your unique touch into each creation. Your kitchen is your canvas, and "Kiwi Jam Delights" is your companion on this flavorful adventure. Cheers to the endless possibilities that await as you continue to explore the delectable world of kiwi-inspired preserves!